All Scripture references taken from the KJV unless otherwise indicated.

Do Not Work for Money by Dr. Marlene Miles

Don't Refuse Me, Lord, Book 1

Lord, Help My Debt, Book 2

As My Soul Prospers, Book 3

Do Not Work for Money, Book 4

Freshwater Press

ISBN# 978-1-893555-90-7

eBook version

Copyright 2022 by Dr. Marlene Miles

All rights reserved. No part of this book may be reproduced, distributed, or transmitted by any means or in any means including photocopying, recording or other electronic or mechanical methods without prior written permission of the publisher except in the case of brief publications or critical reviews.

Table of Contents

Do Not Work for Money 4
Minding My Business 8
Spiritual Housekeeping 14
Networking 17
Look *Past* the Board 20
Do You Want Me or Not? 27
Not Knowing Who You Are 34
Money & Holiness 36
Great Prosperity 42
Just Ask Him 45
Love or Money 52
Such & Such 59
Liar, Liar 65
Stupid Money--*Money in Rebellion* 74
Spiritual Transference 77
Money in Dominion 82
Unconsecrated Money 87
Knock Mammon Off the Throne 96
Consecrated Money 98
Financial Terrorism 100
Financial Warfare 106
Wellth 115
Dear Reader: 117

Christian books by this author..........................117

Do Not Work for Money

Freshwater Press, USA

Do Not Work for Money

Those who want to get rich fall into temptation and a trap and into many foolish and harmful desires that plunge people into ruin and destruction (1Timothy 6:9 NIV).

How many folks have you heard say that they'd give their right arm or some other body part for something? Don't say that. It's not cute, it's not clever, and it is extremely dangerous. I ain't giving up no body parts for material success, and neither should you. Do not work solely for money; do not make money a *god*. Do not trade any part of your life, body or soul for wealth, riches, fame. Those are devil deals.

Every time we speak, angels are listening. Which angels? Depends on if you're saved and your relationship with God. That is if you're saved and have a relationship with God, then God's angels are listening and prepared to make what you have spoken, in faith, and especially in repetition, for your life.

If you are not saved, outside of God's Mercy, your proclamations are to the *god* of this world, Satan, who also has fallen angels (demons) waiting to make the evil, dumb, stupid, rebellious, unwise thing that you spoke, come to pass in your life. It may not happen quickly enough for you to remember you said that and then it happened; but for the most part, you said that, and then it happened.

Have you ever considered that many who have experienced great successes have also suffered great losses? Could it be their big mouths and the devil deals they've made--, unknowingly with their not so clever, but I think I'm so clever mouths? We are all making deals all day, and sometimes at night as well. Pray they are not devil deals.

People, someone is always listening. Listening, and recording the details of your wants, desires, lusts, and needs. Even ***creating*** the need to make you crave it all the more.

Don't work for money. Once it is known that you will work, or do anything for money, the devil will stick close to you, even sending a guardian demon to compromise you, initiate, trick, or trap you into his princedom. He is the *prince* of this world, the *prince* of the powers of the air; he is NOT a king. He is a *prince* and therefore has a princedom.

Make no mistake, if you work for money the devil will make his offer to you with money as the bait. That doesn't mean that you'll get money, either any money or enough money, or that you'll get to enjoy or keep it. It only means that you've indicated what lure the devil should put on his hook as he goes fishing for your soul.

Okay, if you work, shouldn't you get paid? Yes. But we all need to be doing the work that God has assigned us to do as our purpose for being here. Once a person indicates that they will do anything for money, the devil will offer them **money**, usually a counterfeit **offer**. If they accept**, knowingly, or unknowingly,** the devil will put them to work doing what the devil wants them to do, or anything *other* than what God wants them to do. In this way, they waste time, they waste purpose, they waste their life, and they waste destiny.

Money was the bait.

This is why we have to acknowledge God, especially in our life's work so we will fulfill purpose, and destiny. This will most often put us in right places at the right time, making divine connections and in position to receive blessings that are commanded by God for us.

The blessings of the LORD maketh rich and he addeth no sorrow with it. Proverbs 10:22

Work in the field that interests you. Work in the environment you enjoy. Work with people you enjoy. Work for profit. Be led by God, the Spirit of God and in wise counsel with people who are also Spirit-filled and Spirit-led.

People who work for money make money a god and they let money pull them around by the nose.

Minding My Business

Don't refuse, me Lord. I want to be in business for myself.

First, evaluate why you want to be in or own a business. Do you want to be your own boss, or is it to boss others around? Do you have a desire to bring a good or service to market that no one has seen before, such as a God-idea? Do you have a desire to be a blessing? Prestige? Or is it all about money? You want to be rich?

Money

If self-employed make sure you have right motives, mainly that you are not working just for money. If you are saved chances are very good that you are not working for money, although carnal Christians is a real thing.

In your enterprise, if at all possible, do not hire people who only work for money. People who work for money will never make enough money; or it they do; they will simply quit showing up to work. They are not easily or ever satisfied because they're always looking to see how much others are making. They even want to know what *you* **are** taking home. You who shoulders the burdens, have all the headaches and have to solve all the problems--, they are worried about what *you* earn or net from **your** business.

Those are the ones who most often cannot be trusted. They may decide to take their pay into their own hands, stealing, cheating the time clock, or they begin grumbling and interfering with team spirit and company morale.

The best workers, employees I've ever had:

- caught the vision of the house,
- worked without regard to pay or benefits.
- contributed to the efficiency, productivity and joyfulness of the workplace. I can't help but give them increases and perks. It's a joy.

I have never had an employee, whom I've kept under my employ, who ever had to ask me for a raise. That is if they last as my employee.

Excellent reasons to want to be self-employed.

- To work for yourself, to your own satisfaction, control your own pay, and the joy of success.
- To provide a new, or unusual, useful service or product.
- To provide something that people need, enjoy, or have to have. To solve a problem or problems.
- God has given you a purpose and a destiny-related directive to be self-employed or start your own business. What God has told you to do can only be achieved if you are self-employed.

Do work that you enjoy. If you don't like selling, don't get into sales, even if you see others making millions in that field. If you dislike your job, you won't be successful. Success is measured in more than money. If you hate your work, it will hate you right back. How then will you get up in the mornings? You would begrudge skipping lunch if you had to. You will find that you can't wait to get home. You'll be inefficient and unproductive because your mind will be on how *not* to work, instead of doing your work.

Money is a byproduct, but do not work for money, but do work for profit. Make profit (money) a goal, not a *god*. Maintain the space between the A and the L in *goal* do not make money your *god*.

Do not work for money.

Get a clear picture of the enterprise you will be in. Do your research. Check with God as well as man on this. What's the present state of this type of business? What's the future of this type of business?

1. Is this for the long term or do you work it for a couple of years then sell it?
2. What are your plans for this business that you want God to bless?
3. Get someone else to run it, or sell it after you've built it up?

The glory comes after, not before. Be patient. Don't go buy new stuff until you actually get paid.

4. How much work? How many hours will you have to actually work to get it going?

5. How many dishes will you have to or you willing to wash in your own restaurant while you're waiting for it to become very successful?

Do work that you're called to do.

You will automatically enjoy doing the work that you're called to do. God has placed certain skills, gifts, talents, and abilities in you for your life's work and prosperity. When you do the things that He has called and purposed you to do, you will find prosperity. Find out what they are. Take a spiritual gifts discovery, it's an excellent gauge of your spiritual giftedness. Once you complete a discovery, couple the spiritual gifts information with prayer, counseling, talent, skills, hobbies and interests to arrive at your purpose. Also, you must try things until you find the thing or things that you know you're supposed to be doing. Work sequentially to be led to discovering your purpose and proving it, walking in it. The most successful job you can ever do is God's purpose for you to do when He put you here.

Discern the Time

If you need to hurry to get your product on the market in your area, then do it. Don't miss the window of opportunity because of procrastination, and don't miss your time because of money. Be creative with finances. If a bank turns you down, seek another channel such as parents, friends, relatives, associates, associations, SBA grants. Borrow it from yourself. Borrow it from your retirement plan to keep your day job until your new enterprise kicks off and pay yourself back in a timely fashion.

Don't sell your dreams or share them with people whom you do not absolutely trust. Don't tell your dreams to people who don't understand. They may try to talk you out of good ideas that God has given you.

Spiritual Housekeeping

Give; it's the top spiritual law of money.

Just as the Queen of Sheba came with gifts for Solomon, the saint or sinner can come with gifts to give of his wealth, (1 Kings 10:1-14). As we Christians give, we do expect a return in our giving. But we can do more than just give to get a return. Let's say we get a bill in the mail and then decide to give an offering to God in order to get enough money to pay the bill. Then we may have certainly acted in faith, but if we look *past* the ability to get that bill paid, what is there? Praise and **glory that is due to God.**

When we live, give, act in faith and God blesses, people will see our lifestyle. People will see how the church really lives, how we *represent*. People will see how the church, the individual members really live by faith and by our example, by our ministry, others will be drawn to church, to the Kingdom of God, all to the glory of God.

Give with:

- Clean hands.
- Right heart.

Get the Accursed thing out of the Camp

Get the accursed thing, the tithe, out of the camp. Plant seed where you're being fed. Name your seed. Say what you want over your business. Speak good things and success over your ideas and treat them right. Then you'll get new and greater ideas.

Speak good things over your employees and staff, whether the good people have applied to work with you yet, or not. Speak well over staff, employees until good things manifest.

Do not work for money.

For the love of money is the root of all evil, which while some coveted after. They have erred from the faith and pierced themselves through with many sorrows. (1 Timothy 6:10).

But do work for profit and increase.

Go to Work

New businesses are like babies. You have to carry them sometimes. Push them at other times and wipe up little messes before they become big ones. Get up, get to the office on time. No lollygagging or sitting around the house as though you're some big shot. Big shots usually only shoot once. That's why they're so big. Let your discipline show; that will inspire staff as well. Soon your business will function without making a mess at all.

Networking

Real networking may not be what you think. Jesus sent the Disciples to a man who had a donkey on which He could ride into Jerusalem. Else He would have had to go see a man who knew a man who knew a person who could do Him a favor. We think the latter is networking, but real networking is after having heard the Word of God. Especially regarding prosperity. Jesus told the fishermen to let down their Nets. They had the greatest catch ever. That's networking. When God tells you to let down your net, whatever your net is, He will prosper you greatly. Your net could be your own shoe repair business, bakery or business consulting firm. Whatever it is, your net is your own business. Whatever God has put on your heart to do. Work with diligence and regularity. It is the work that you do to honor Him. It is the work you honor Him by doing. And you honor Him with the offerings of the increase of that business. That work, job or business is your **net**.

However, if you don't have a net, you can't let one down. When God has a motherlode of fish or other prosperity to give you, what is the channel or channels by which He can flow? OK, you work in the mailroom, have for the past 15 years. You have a supervisor, a foreman, a manager, 3 associate VP's, two junior VP's over you, before you get to the senior VP who works for the CEO. God can do it, He can bless you through that complex channel, but it is far more difficult for Him than being able to speak to you and say, **"LET DOWN YOUR NET."**

Your net is your own thing, your own business, or even a part-time enterprise (side hustle) that you enjoy where you use your God-given skills and abilities to work to earn a living, bless others and be a blessing.

I am not telling you to quit your job. Only God can do that. Nor has He told me to tell you to quit your job. He has told me to tell you to get yourself a *net*.

Maybe God isn't refusing you. There are just too many obstacles, too many double agents posing as *people,* in the way. You've got to take right and godly action to remove obstacles. Daniel did it, (Daniel 9).

Exercise:

6. Why do I work?
7. Do I have a *net*? If so, what is it?
8. If not, why? Why not?

Seek divine Wisdom to find out what your **net** is or what it should be.

Hint: It is completely related to your purpose.

9. I expect to have a **net** to let down by what date?

Look *Past* the Board

I was in the dojo, dressed and ready for the Taekwondo board breaking competition. Two black belts were sturdily holding a 2-inch-thick board. I took the stance, then kicked, yelling, *"Kyop!"*

Nothing happened to the board--, couldn't believe it didn't break. My heel turned red and begin to throb, which didn't help my anger or embarrassment that the board didn't break because there were onlookers.

Remembering that the instructor told me to look **past the board**, to kick **past the board**. He said to envision what was *behind* the board and kick that. Run that past me again. Kick what's *behind* the board? The two black belts knew; I had yet to find out.

Okay, rethinking this... what's behind the board? Air. What was behind and beyond the board? Nothing. No. Air. Yes. And what else?

Here's a good opportunity to use faith. You know that thing in Hebrews 11:1?

> The substance of things hoped for, the evidence of things not seen, (Hebrews 11:1).

The Cloak

Behind the board is air. Nothing. Or better-- *things not seen*. The things not seen in the natural can only be seen by faith. Behind the board is the prince of the powers of the air and his workers.

In times long past, the famous gentleman Sir Walter Raleigh, took off his cloak to cover over a mud puddle for a lady. If I were that lady taking a step instead of making a martial arts kick, and the cloak was not there, I would still be considering where I would place my foot. The Gentleman of God called the Holy Spirit may be doing that for us, as well; He may be cloaking things as not to let us see all the things that lurk in the spirit world, because those things might scare us. God cloaks the ugly, the scary and the unsavory for us all the time. And thank God the Cloak, too, is invisible. If we really could see what we are stepping on, spiritually speaking, we might not step.

The Word says that we shall tread on scorpions, serpents, bruising the heads of snakes, young adders among other things. **How do we know that we aren't doing that in every holy step we make each day?** Could be why our feet hurt at the end of each day and some days more than others. Could be why the devil hates us VERTICAL and attacks us while we are horizontal.

We could be warriors extraordinaire in the spirit as to why those dogs are howling at night and those shoes come off as soon as we hit the door in the evenings from work. If I could really see what I was kicking, I might not kick.

This is why we must walk by faith. We don't need to <u>*see*</u> everything. Just as you don't tell your kid that the "beef" you're having for dinner is really liver until after he tries it the first time and likes it. Similarly, God may not let you see that devil, you've just defeated until **after** you've defeated it. Selah.

So we step by faith, not by sight. What are we stepping on? Scorpions. Serpents, young adders, lions and things that might bite us were it possible. If some of us were to see those things, or even the cloak that covers them, we might move out of faith, into fear, then some of those things with teeth and stingers, might actually get us.

WARNING: Only close your eyes if you're moving in faith. If not, keep those eyes open so in the natural you can protect yourself somewhat. Without faith, it is impossible to please God. So when you're not in faith, God can't help you very much anyway. Better do what you can for yourself. Remember, when you're in faith, you do not rely on sight.

That is why it is impossible to walk, step or kick without faith. Most people without faith only stand still, crawl or lie down and get trampled on.

Behold, I've given to you power to tread on serpents and scorpions and other, and over the power of the enemy, and nothing by any means shall hurt you,
(Luke 10:19).

... Back to the board breaking —

Christians step and kick daily, so I can do this!

By faith, behind the board is the heel of my foot, the sole of my foot, and God gives me victory where the sole of my foot treads, (Joshua 1:3). Following the instruction to kick past the board, I raise my leg and with new vision and purpose to break that board, I proclaim, *"Kyop!"*

It broke.

If what you're looking at is not God, then it's an obstacle. Look *past* it.

If what I'm looking at is not God, then I need to change my focus. I need to look *past* the obstacle. What's there? God will take care of, or help me remove the obstacles that try to put themselves between me and Him. Every problem, event or obstacle is just a distraction to keep my mind and eyes off God. Then I will always be victorious by keeping my mind stayed on Him and my eyes fixed past the hills, past the boards.

Past the Board

Currently at our church we have a fundraising board. We look at it and imagine how great it would be to reach that top number. But

God is saying *look past the board*. What is *past* the board is our newly acquired land, our family life center and salvation of many youth and lost souls.

The glory of God is *past the board*. The glory comes *after*. The glory of the father is the son; the son comes *after*. The glory of the woman is her long hair; the hair comes *after*. The glory of the cake is the icing; the icing comes after. The glory comes **after**.

So past the board is the glory of breaking it. Past the fundraising board is the success of reaching the top number that we want for our church's ministry. The real glory is past the board, past that top number, and we see past the board by faith.

If we just look **at** the board, if, we just look **at** the bill, if, we just look *at* the problem it can all become a stumbling block. It can be magnified in our imaginations to more than an obstacle to be kicked down, knocked down, stepped on, pulled down, or taken down. Look ***past*** the board, past the mountain or obstacles and see what God has for you. Remember what God has promised you.

He hasn't changed His mind. Look past the board so God can bless your **faith** and get His glory.

Faith sees *past* what is seen.

The purpose of things seen is to minister to man's flesh. The devil perverts this and uses things seen to obstruct the spiritual. Distraction is enemy tactic number one.

God gives us victories over potential distractions by.

Cloaking the ugly, then revealing the spiritual when we're ready.

Exercise:

10. What has God graciously cloaked for me in the past?
11. What's on my board now?
12. What's past my board now?
13. What do I need to look around or past to see God?

Do You Want Me or Not?

Are you behaving as someone who wants money or whatever you're asking God for? When God looks at you, what does He see? Does He see a person who really believes God will answer and who is able to *receive*? Do you have any idea how to *receive*? Do you have any experience *receiving*?

In football they have a special guy who knows how to do that better than anybody else: a receiver. The team actually has usually four and up to six receivers on their roster on game day. They need specialists at this because many people don't know how to receive.

Could it be that the Kingdom of God has so many people who have been taught and retaught how to be *givers* that there are not enough *receivers*? Giving is a spiritual gift; and it is the first law of money and substance. God taught it to Cain and Abel in the Garden at Eden.

Shouldn't there be a corresponding or correlating spiritual gift of *receiving*? We've all been beat over the head with being *more blessed to give than receive*. That Scripture does not say it is **only** blessed to give. Nor does it say it is unblessed to *receive*.

The economy of God is based on both giving and receiving. Else, sow and reap wouldn't work. We just put our seeds in the ground and that would be that, like the man with the one Talent, who did nothing with it and simply returned the same one Talent to God. This did not please God. Maybe this man didn't know how to *receive* and **knew** that he didn't know how.

If we were only to give, the principle of planting and harvesting would only be planting.

We would only *give* a cup of water. We would not drink any. We would give food to the needy, but we wouldn't eat anything. We would not *receive* nourishment for our natural health.

God gave us Jesus Christ for the remission of our sins and Eternal Life. If we were not to receive, we wouldn't receive Salvation, Adoption,

Forgiveness, Justification, Redemption, and 30-, 60-, and 100-fold returns in the Offering. We **must receive**. If we do not, we would only give our life to Christ, but not receive Eternal Life or Abundant Life in return. If we weren't dead from the previous paragraph, we'd certainly be dead by the end of this one.

For the very stubborn, if we were only to *give* but never receive, we would exhale but never inhale. Now who's dead?

Didn't God receive Jesus back to Himself, proclaiming Him as the first of many brethren? Yes, God gave Jesus and received Him back. **If giving and receiving didn't work, God would have given Jesus and would *receive* no other sons and daughters to Himself.** And we all know that's not the case.

Too many of us have packed our spiritual bags set for glory. It's too soon; there's still plenty of work to do. Why work? Because you *received* spiritually, you received spiritual gifts, and now you have to **give**, John said freely you have received, now freely give.

See, you really do know how to receive. You have received Salvation, but you can't leave the planet yet.

Receiving Money

Many don't know how to receive anything from a compliment to a favor, to cash money, and blessings from God. That attitude about receiving things can keep God refusing you; if He sees you're not ready, then you're just not ready. You're supposed to be prospering your soul to be ready, but are you? You are supposed to be improving your mind and attitude about giving and receiving.

Folks have always bellyached and complained about money. How many times have you heard people referring to money as an elusive thing? How many times have they ascribed the ability to earn, receive, and have money as a quality of *other people* rather than themselves? **Why do people give that blessing away, sometimes to people they don't even like?** How many times have you said, "There you go, Mr. Moneybags, you've always got a pocket full"?

How many times have you had things like that said to you? And when it was said to you, how did you handle it? Try this, *"Thank you, God is faithful."*

Or, "My God supplies all my needs according to His riches in glory. Amen." Anything else is rejecting the money, prosperity, and blessing. Like the traveling salesman, if you reject him long enough, he will stop knocking on your door. In the case of the salesman, maybe that's good. In the case of a blessing from God, it's not.

Attitudes About Money

Your attitude and words about money, health or healing could be repelling just what you ask for, want, and need.

Hard Earned

If you believe and especially say that money is hard earned, then it will be hard to earn. God says we can reap and enjoy the fruits of our labor. God says that what we set our hands to do, He will prosper. Money should not be hard to earn if you're doing what God tells you to do. In the right season, you will reap. If you acknowledge Him, He will direct your ways and give you all things that pertain to life and godliness.

Fear of Success

Are you really sure you want success, or do you keep finding excuses not to do the thing that you know will take you to the next level?

Guilt

Do you experience the guilt of I-have-and others-don't? If you are experiencing the divine favor of God, enjoy it. Favor is not fair, but God is just. If it's your season to prosper, then prosper and give God His glory.

Are you worried that people will worry you for money, loans, and favors if you have wealth? Do you think you might feel better, or have more friends if you also don't have? Thoughts and emotions like that repel blessings.

There must always be a balance of giving and receiving.

Mediocrity

You might be thinking or saying that you'll have more friends if you are average like they are. That's why you made that C on purpose in high school history when you could have made an A. I personally have more "friends" when I was average than when I made straight A's. I had more friends when fatter than when a size 6. You might also be saying that the middle of the road, mainstream and average, seems to work in life. Maybe it does, but that's neither God's plan nor His best for you.

If God were planning to bless mediocrity, He would just do that. God said about Jesus, ***This is My Son in whom I am well pleased."*** He did **<u>not</u>** say, This is My Son and He's okay, average.

There are millions and millions of seemingly average folks with awesome, unstirred and untapped gifts, talents, and abilities in them. But God didn't put gifts in us to lie dormant. God wants to bless the extraordinary. He causes us to do great exploits. He blesses the person with *extra* courage, *extra* faith, and *extra* boldness to walk in what's right and fully use all he has been given.

God will not refuse the man who has come to the end of himself and is now looking to God. Refusals from God come when you can do it yourself, but you haven't tried, stirred, or tapped, when you haven't used, tried to use, or properly used what you already have.

Not Knowing Who You Are

The devil has so many so confused that if God handed you a spiritual mirror and showed you the reflection of yourself as He sees you, you probably will be startled. You might wonder who that was standing near or behind you, causing that reflection in the mirror, not knowing ***that's supposed to be you.***

Not knowing that you're supposed to have money, abundance, or wealth is one of those things that, if you don't know about it you might remain without those things.

If you only take your cues from people to whom you are related or spend time with, then you will stay at ***their same level***. If that level is low or average, that's exactly where you will be, because that is exactly what you will expect. Based on your gender, race, or background, you may have preconceived notions about how unsuccessful you are to be in life. You've got to erase all that if you're in Christ. Because if you're in Christ, you can go far and above your own imaginings. The successes promised to us, and great successes are not just for those of the *other* gender, or another race, with more education, or of a different cultural background. If you are in Christ, then good success is for you.

Discernment

Use discernment so you don't fall for cons and get rich quick schemes. Discernment is God-given, and it improves by use. The more you use it, the sharper you will get.

Sympathy

People may be able to swindle you out of well-deserved blessings and successes if you fall for false sympathy ploys. If you cannot see through deceitful emotional acts. If you don't have courage enough to say, *"No,"* this could be why God has refused you so far. He knows you will lose it, give it all away, or could be duped out of it.

Money & Holiness

Refusing money trying to appear holy will keep money away from you. Stop saying, *"No, you don't have to give me anything,"* or *"That's all right,"* when someone wants to pay you, and then wonder why God isn't blessing you. God sends blessings through **people**. By refusing people, and trying to appear nice, kind, or holy, you may be refusing the exact channel that God has set up to bless you. I'm never surprised by how much even a short taxi ride cost in most cities. If you're giving someone a ride and they want to give you $5 or $10 and you know they can afford it, accept it, unless the Holy Spirit says not to.

Traveling only four miles by taxi cost us $30 on a recent ministry trip. Refusing blessings, trying to appear nice may be quenching the channel that God has set in place to prosper you. Just as the Scriptures say that sometimes you may entertain angels unaware, you may also entertain the person who has your financial or other blessings, unaware. Divine connections are made with *people*. Destiny helpers can be angelic and spiritual, but they can be **PEOPLE** who God has placed in your path to work along with you, albeit for a season, to bless you and help you fulfill purpose and destiny. If you are praying, D*on't refuse me, Lord;* then don't refuse people and the help of people that God may have sent to bless you.

While we shouldn't do favors for people expecting compensation, be open to the fact that God can bless you anytime in any way through anyone He chooses. He's God. Don't block God's flow.

Many have entertained or disdained the person who has their blessing--, *Unawares.*

Don't refuse every time someone offers, then you won't have to go back and rehearse how much you did for that person when their car was in the shop, for example. When they don't do something you want them to do next year don't declare that they *owe* you. If that's the case, then it's a sign that you **should have accepted the money** that they offered to pay you when you gave them a ride that day. That was their way of _completing_ the transaction. When you refused, **you** completed the transaction, your way--, as a favor or a gift, receiving no pay.

Maybe you were planning a different, better, or more lucrative blessing for yourself, (for God to send you). But when that didn't happen, you may feel that God or the other person still _owes_ you. Sorry, the transaction was completed. If you provided the favor, hoping for their undying praise and loyalty instead of $10 for the gas and time, you should have told them before you took them across town that the price was undying praise and loyalty. Sorry, the transaction is completed, and you refused your reward. We've all done this at some time or other. That's why I ask, do you really know how and when to _receive_? I am not saying that $10 will make you prosperous, but it speaks to your _attitude_ about receiving. If you won't receive $10, then how can you receive $500, or even more?

Perhaps God wants you to get paid for a service you can perform or a good that you can create that could be your own lucrative or prosperous _business_--, your own **net.** But if you always turn people down when they want to pay you, then you cannot make that into a business.

For instance, a woman makes very lovely baked goods, but she always gives them away. People have offered to pay her for years. She won't accept it. She could be a very successful baker, but she's not, by her own choice. It's not God.

Have enough Grace and **humility** to accept a gift, especially a monetary gift, from a Godly source when you really need it. Pride will make you put your hand up and say, *No thank you* to a $5,000 check from a millionaire.

Making Room

If you are not making room for the abundance that God has for you, then you don't really know Him. Or you don't believe that He will really bless you.

… For now the Lord hath made room for us, and we shall be fruitful in the land. (Genesis 26:22b)

God makes room for us, and in so doing He makes room for us to be fruitful and blessed. In turn, we need to make room for Him to bless us.

When you have faith, you will make room for the blessings that God has for you. If God sees you're not ready, He will not let His incredible gift just run off the edges or go to waste. He is looking for people to bless, but He is not desperate.

Wise Management

And why stewardship? Because things have to be organized and planned. What is this money or whatever you want from God *for*? God gives very detailed plans. In building He gave exact to the cubit measurements to the Israelites. He also specified color, fabric, style, and ornamentation. That's God's way when it comes to stewardship or anything else. He is meticulous. Your pastor is not being impossible about the plan or vision that God has given him; he's being obedient. That's why God gave a plan to him and not to you. God knew whom He could trust with details. None of us are in any position to try to change **God's plan;** therefore, listen to the man of God. Listen to the man who is listening to God, if you are not listening to God.

To be a wise steward, you must know the plan of God or follow closely the person to whom

God has revealed the vision--, your pastor, your leader, or the head of your committee. When you have sought God for all these particulars, listened and studied to show yourself approved, faithful, and disciplined, He can't help but bless you. God will not refuse when you are prepared and have ***made room*** for His great abundance and blessings.

Great Prosperity

God is asking, *You say you love Me, but do you want Me or not?* If you refuse Salvation, then you've refused God. Too many want health and prosperity without God. That's not honoring God and it's not really possible. Many receive Salvation and also want and are willing to receive health but refuse wealth because they've tied poverty and holiness together.

Do you want God or not? Do you want what He has to offer, or not? These things all come together, but many behave as though they themselves decide which ones are holy, but that has already been decided--, by God. He has packaged them all together for your life and godliness. God is expecting you to be in health and prosper, even as your soul prospers, (3 John 1:2). So He's still asking, *Do you want me or not? All of Me, or not?*

Whatever is from God is holy.

Do you want God or just His stuff? You can't rob God. You can't have God's *stuff* without God. You may be able to take it or steal it from one of His children, but you can't take it from God, and you won't keep it. God's got more than one warrior who doesn't mind the confrontation involved in getting God's stuff back.

Don't refuse me, Lord. Then don't refuse His lordship. Make sure Jesus is the Lord of your life. Don't refuse me, Lord. Have you been refusing His blessings all of your life? Have you been refusing His gifts? You know, the gifts that He has sent you through *people*. Then what's going to make God answer you favorably now?

Exercise:

14. Repent of ever refusing God.
15. Make room worksheet. I make room for these things in my life because I really believe God.
16. From the word.
    a. _____
    b. _____

    c. _____

17. From his voice to me.

    a. _____

    b. _____

    c. _____

18. From prophetic words I have received.

    a. _____

    b. _____

    c. _____

19. From dreams.

    a. _____
    _____

    b. _____

20. From the desires of my heart. Things I have prayed for:

    a. _____

    b. _____
    _____

I make room for the things for which I believe God.

Just Ask Him

Asking out of order, or asking amiss (James 4:25), is one of the main reasons that Christians don't receive things from God. Many are trying to be 'good' Christians based on what they think Christianity is. Are we trying to be liked, or trying not to appear greedy when we *don't ask for things we really need and want,* and trying to appear holy and humble? We may not be really honest in our prayer time to God, in public or in private.

Tradition

One of the reasons may be that church tradition is to put poverty and holiness together. That is not what God intends. God owns all the silver, all the gold and all the cattle on a thousand hills, and God is still HOLY. There's no shortage of wealth in the Earth. Further, God is looking for people to bless; He is looking for people to give favor and wealth to.

We want, we have needs, we have desires, and we sometimes feel desperate. While saying that God has promised us desires of our heart, too many of us don't even ask God for the things we really want.

Delight thyself also in the Lord, and he shall give thee the desires of thine heart. (Psalms 37:4)

God knows my heart may be your rationale. Then you may add to that, *"When He wants me to have _____(whatever), He'll send it."* Faithful, but foolish.

Fear & Self Loathing

Sometimes, knowingly, or unknowingly. We ask for part of what we want. We ask for the *nice* parts of what we want. We asked for the parts that seem acceptable to people we know. They seem like churchy and godly things to ask for. In times past, a traditional request was for *portion of health*. Excuse me; I want more than a portion; I want to be whole. I want divine health. What kind of health did Jesus have? Jesus wasn't languishing away with arthritis or other illnesses or diseases.

So many times we don't **really** ask for what we want. You might ask for something similar or something *like* the thing you want, because if you look around you might not see anybody else with the things you really desire. Nobody else at your church has a $1,000,000 house. Nobody else you *know* has a $1,000,000 house. If that's what you want, for a Godly purpose, ask for it.

Picture a Monopoly game with houses, hotels, lands, and et cetera. Now make it real. God owns **all** of it. You can have any and all of the things you see, but instead you only ask for a trailer or a studio apartment. Why? You could have a Rolls Royce or a Cadillac, but you ask for a Pinto. Why? Is it because you don't think God's got it? No, He's got it. Don't you think you deserve the nice stuff? If you don't, you really don't like or love yourself. Get some teaching and ministry (deliverance) on self-esteem.

If you only ask for things that you know you can have, then that's not using your faith either.

If you don't think you can have what you really want, you may ask for cheap substitutes. And when you get nothing, you may become angry at God.

Yeah, if you receive a cheap copy of something, you'd be angry, unsatisfied. If you're afraid to ask God, then you don't have enough faith, or if you don't know Him. Singles who are afraid to ask for the mate they *really* want may just ask for any old thing, and sometimes that's what they get. Ask for the desires of your heart or something better. Don't ask for something less. Don't say, *"Lord, I just want a husband, any man will do."* No! Don't ask for a ditch digger, a drug dealer, or an almost-reformed alcoholic if that's not what you really want.

Some divorced singles, or those who have been in previous romantic relationships might identify one thing that they just can't stand about their former mate, and they make a vow that they won't put up with that one thing that they hated in the last relationship in the next relationship. For instance, the ex-husband wouldn't work. Now you're on a mission to find a man with a job. That's all you are looking for or asking God for. How about the rest of him? If you just ask God for a man with a job, you just might get it. This man may even be wealthy, but you may be miserable as he showers you with gifts and money. He may become extremely obnoxious, unattractive, or even abusive to you.

Or he may not make very much money at all. What if his job is just a paper route, and he works two hours a day? He's met the requirement of being employed.

When you set limits on God, sometimes you don't get anything. Not because of punishment. God just can't find anything suitable to bless you, based on your ask, expectation, and faith. He doesn't have any half ways or sort of's...

Abide In Me

Ask what you will, and it shall be given when you abide in the Lord. That means that your thought life is in Him too, and those things you think on will be acceptable to Him. The things that are in your heart *will* be pleasing to God, and He will be well-pleased to give them to you. The Scripture below refers to what I call the abiding desires or the abiding requests. If you abide in Him, you won't ask for things that don't line up with His will, His plan, and His purpose for you.

If you abide in me, and my words abide in you, you shall ask what you will, and it shall be done unto you, John 15-7.

Stay in Character

When you ask a child what he wants for his birthday, you expect to hear something imaginative and fun. Perhaps your child is a soccer player, a bike rider and an outdoorsy kind of kid, but he tells you he wants a book as his gift--, that's all he wants. A book.

You look twice to see if something's wrong with the boy. That's what God is doing when you're asking for things that are out of character for you. He knows you want a Range Rover, but you're asking Him for a Yugo. Why would He waste His time giving you something you really don't want? So you don't get anything? That's mercy.

Careful though, sometimes God will give us over to our ridiculous requests. It's happened to me. Recall Chapter 1 of this tome? We get something that we really don't want but we asked for it or said it. It's a hard lesson and not easy to forget.

Just as you would try to talk your child out of a gift that you know he is just trying to *please you* by asking for. God is talking to you. Are you listening?

What Do You Want?

Could it be that you *don't know* what you want? Is it ignorance? Slack of desire? Ignorance of desire?

That woman who Jesus encountered at the well who was on her 5th man seemed not to know what she wanted--, relationship wise.

Love or Money

Would you rather have love or money? Fill in the blank.

I asked a friend that. She took days, maybe weeks, before answering. Then she answered incorrectly. Like the woman at the well, what's the wrong answer? Either is the wrong answer. The correct answer is both. In ignorance, the world poses this question to us, either verbally or non-verbally in the process of living. The correct answer is **both**. Giving one or the other as your answer forces you into a word curse—even if it is a child that is asking you this in "jest", or you were the child who answered one or the other. It still locked you into a word curse. Have you broken it yet?.

God has promised us ***all things*** that pertain to life and godliness. It's the devil that separates the two. Put them back together. **You** put them back together. You can have success, wealth, prosperity, abundance, and enjoy it as well. It is not one or the other.

Seems like God is always refusing you? Maybe God is waiting for you to ask for what you want, what you *really, really* want. God is not a God of half-the-way. He's not a halfway God. So, what happens? Many times, you may not get anything at all. Perhaps He's patiently waiting for you to grow to see the whole vision and not just part of the picture. Maybe God is teaching you and waiting for you to ask for it right and for the right reasons.

Stop being angry at God. He's not doing anything to you. Look at yourself to see what the delay could be.

If you think it's love OR money, you may end up with neither. Are you one of those who think that holiness means wearing dresses longer than your shoes, no makeup, and looking drab or homely? No wonder you can't get anyone to come to church with you. Your looks make Christianity look like a bore. You make it look like a makeover into the spinster's club rather than having relationship with God. Submitting to God does not mean dressing as they did in Bible days.

Further, you won't be very attractive to the opposite gender dressed like that either. No, I'm not saying to show everything you have, but if you think poverty is holiness and dressing drably is holiness then you'll repel both money and men.

Neither does holiness mean waiting for food to fall from the sky and water to flow out of rocks. It doesn't mean that you wander aimlessly until someone gives you a better place to live. Holiness does not mean waiting for a daily miracle in order to exist. Signs are for sinners. Miracles are for desperate situations. That is not where God has called us to live.

Do you think God is saying*? **Look, all you Heavenly Hosts, the desperate ones, they're Mine**. No, God says, **"THE JUST SHALL LIVE BY FAITH."** That means obeying the laws and working the principles of God and having faith that He will help you. He will keep you. We are to live in abundance and overflow, not in poverty.

If you can't live in a nice house, drive a nice car, have money in the bank, investments plus a decent retirement plan, _and_ live in holiness, then you're not living in holiness. *Appearing* to live in holiness won't impress God.

What do I mean? If you had drugs, and would have used them, you are not living in obedience or holiness; you're just doing without.

If you are not stealing because they took you off the cash register at your job, but you **would** steal if it were your day to be the cashier, then you're not holy; you just don't have access.

You're not sinning sexually because you only hang out with the gender you're not attracted to, that's not holiness. That's *please help me so I won't sin* babysitting. That doesn't mean to spend time around the gender you're attracted to in order to prove a point, if you're not yet fully delivered from sex temptations.

Let's bring it home. If you are **not** fasting or overeating because you don't have enough money to buy food, but when you get money for food, you will overeat, poverty is not making you holy, poverty is just depriving you from doing what you really want to do. If because of poverty, you've learned discipline, then that's good.

You learned your alphabets in kindergarten, but did you stay in kindergarten? **Now that you're disciplined, you don't have to stay poor.**

The man who has access to every temptation or former temptation, but does not *desire* to do those things, and is disciplined not to do those things because of his love for and relationship with God is the man who is living in holiness. But the man who is living alone in a cave without television, but wants all manner of worldly things, the man who is suffering without is not necessarily the holy one. As you see, **not having does not mean not *wanting*.** If that were the case, then every homeless person on every street would be holy. Poverty and holiness do not necessarily go together, and there is a real temptation for many people when they get a little money to forget God, or when they get around those temptations that used to get them in trouble, they get right back into the same trouble.

When will we overcome?

If the means or the opportunity is not present, but you still really want to do it--, that's what the penal system is based on. If a person wants to commit a crime, they are physically restrained from committing the crime by being locked up. That may make them *criminally innocent*, but in their heart, they still want to kill, they aren't innocent, nor are they holy. They still sin, although they have not *transgressed*. What is in the heart speaks of who a person really is. Sin is as simple as thinking on it, thinking on it to do it. Taking the action is the transgression. The Bible says that the man who has looked on a woman to sin has already sinned. He may not have transgressed, but he has sinned. If, like the criminal in the jail, he is locked into his daily and family routine and can't get away to actually do the deed, he has not transgressed, but he has indeed sinned. That man or woman is naturally innocent but spiritually guilty. He needs to repent.

Poor to distraction is a trick of the enemy.

If you are living in poverty and without creature comforts, there will certainly be temptations. Stealing just to eat is not holy. It is not holy to starve to death.

The sane man knows, *No.*

When you are so poor that you are distressed, distracted from serving God and attending to the things of God, then you're living in defeat, and you are so poor that you can all you can think about is how poor you are. Then you are still living a defeated life. When you are so poor that all you think about is money, from the lack of it to the lust for it, you're still defeated by the enemy. God does not want you thinking about money all day long. When will you give time to Him? Pray that God will give you enough. Just ask Him.

> Remove far from me vanity and lies: give me neither poverty nor riches; feed me with food convenient for me:
>
> Lest I be full, and deny thee, and say, Who is the LORD? or lest I be poor, and steal, and take the name of my God in vain. Proverbs 30:8-9

Such & Such

> And I gave thee thy masters house, thy masters wives into thy bosom, and gave thee the House of Israel and Judah. And if that had been too little. I'm, moreover, would have given unto thee such and such things. 2 Samuel 12:8

God just wants you to ask Him; just ask Him. In faith, we are to ask God for the things we want—the things we *really* want. He has said He will give us the desires of our heart. What does that mean to you? For King David it was a number of things, and God was faithful to bless him abundantly. God gave David at least four things for slaying Goliath. To me that means that working for God, especially going to get God's stuff back, or protecting God's people pays as well or better than any other kind of work you can do.

> And I gave thee thy masters house, thy masters wives into thy bosom, and gave thee the House of Israel and Judah. And if that had been too little. I moreover, would have given unto thee such and such things.
>
> 2 Samuel 12:8

The Master's House

God gave King David his master's house. The house you used to *serve* in means that God has reversed your slavery, your captivity, your servanthood. God has reversed your bondage, setting you free.

If that weren't enough, He turns around and gives you the mansion on the hill, that house that you used to *admire*. You may have even worked there, polishing the fittings and furnishings, cleaning the windows, or planting gardens, mowing the lawn, taking care of it as though it were yours--, diligently.

Diligence has its own rewards.

Now here it is. He just gave it to you, (Luke 16:12). Thank you, Jesus. You have turned my captivity.

The Master's Wives

God told David he had given him his master's wives. That means *intimate things*. God has given you as a prize for your obedience, discipline, service, and because of your relationship, your master's wives. If you're a man or a woman, it doesn't matter, these wives represent God having given you **people t**o minister to you and your needs. Wives are known as helpmates, destiny helpers. Just as you have served, now you shall *be* served. He has put people in your path to assist you in accomplishing the things you need to get done in your life.

You now have divine favor when you go places. People go out of their way to assist you and to help you succeed. That's God.

Not only that, but you will also humiliate your former captor by having what he had as yours, whether tangible goods or his servants. They are all spoils, and God gives them to the victor. Former master's things, his prized possessions have now become as spoils of war. You have just earned all manner of valuable things as God declares you victor of the battles.

All that the enemy used against you, all that he flaunted in your face, is now yours to use with wise spiritual discretion. God has released you from captivity and bondage and endowed you with high blessings.

The Thrones of Israel and Judah

These Thrones represent heavenly and earthly power. With great benevolence God shows you divine favor and gives you **authority, position,** and **power.** He gives you the Thrones of Israel and Judah.

Christ, who is in the lineage of David and of the Tribe of Judah, sits on the Throne of heavenly power. Salvation belongs to God and Christ in you is the hope of glory.

Life

The other tribes, which comprised the balance of the people of God, represent earthly power. God is giving you all these things that pertain to life and godliness. He's giving you all the things you need to be in power and authority in earthly *and* Heavenly realms.

What Else Do You Want?

Forget the monopoly game. Instead, think of the vastness of the infiniteness of God. What else do you want? Think of the awesomeness of God, then ponder, if you must, why He's asking you, *"What else do you want?"* There are reasons for that question. Consider the following:

- There's more for you than all that He has already given you.
- He wants you to have more than just that.
- He wants to know if you're satisfied.
- He wants to know that you *can be* satisfied.

If God would go through the trouble of asking you, ***What else do you want?*** Then you should be honored to serve such a God. He's telling you that He would have given you ***such and such*** if you had asked Him. It's scriptural, ***such and such*** is in the Bible, (KJV). And that's a whole lot of stuff. ***Such and such*** encompasses everything you can think of and everything that your heart desires. The things that we ask God for, that we think are such big things, are really little things to God. As long as we abide in Him, God says that whatever we ask for, He will give it to us. Jesus says if we ask in His Name, He will give it to us that the Father may be glorified.

But if you never ask Him, if you feel you just can't ask Him. Feeling that it would be wrong, unholy or non-religious to ask Him will get you nothing, outside of Mercy and miracles. Surely, you need to take a long, hard look at your relationship with God. Do you want to be religious like the Sadducees and the Pharisees, or do you want *relationship*?

God cannot use you as a channel of blessing like He did with Abraham, until **you** get satisfied, until you get used to having and being around prosperity, plenty, and abundance. You will consume whatever you receive on your own lust if you're not used to anything. Especially if God gives it to you to distribute to others you can't spend it on or hoard it up for yourself.

Liar, Liar

But the fearful and unbelieving in the abominable murderers and warmongers and sorcerers, and idolaters. And all liars shall have their part in the lake that burneth with fire and brimstone, which is the second death. Revelations 21:8

Do holy people really ask God for material things? Yes, they do. If I'm not asking God for what I really want, then am I an honest person?

What Do *I* Lie About?

The speed limit is 55, why are you doing 70 mph?

That's not lying, is it? You have to be *talking* to lie, right? Wrong, liar, liar, soul's on fire. Someone may present you with a watch, a television or a purse to buy and it's a great deal, but actually it's hot--, stolen. Do you buy it? When you buy stolen goods criminally, it makes you an accessory, and spiritually it makes you a thief.

If God can't trust you with the little things, you might as well forget the big things. The tithe is no different than the honor parking lot, in that if we don't pay the money because we're afraid of getting towed, that's not an honor, that's fear. We should pay it because of honor.

If you don't exceed the speed limit because you're afraid of getting a ticket, you're honoring the authority of the traffic police more than God. Is a traffic ticket worse than eternal damnation, spiritually?

Sane man, what do you say?

Liar, liar. Traffic tickets are for behavior modification, to maintain peace, and safety in the sinners of the world. We are subject to civil laws and tickets them because we are in the world, but we are not *of* the world. Christians are to submit to a higher authority and a higher code of behavior. The goal in driving, for example, is not to avoid the ticket, it is to reach your destination safely. It can be accomplished if you stay under authority, which means obey the laws. Civil laws are the bare minimum and are in place to protect us from sinners, as we should be operating in grace not having to be told all day every day how to conduct ourselves. But do we? Really? Unless we are walking by the Spirit, those civil laws now protect us from sinners as much as it protects sinners from *us*.

I just couldn't ask God for anything; I'm too holy.

Not knowing from one day to the next what you're going to eat and what your children are going to wear to school, or if you've got enough money to pay the house payment is stressful, and it is not the abundant life that Jesus came for us to have. What is so holy about that? God has promised us all things that pertain to life and Godliness. If you don't know that, then you're not holy enough. If you don't know that God wants you to be blessed and give you the desires of your heart then you don't know Him. What's so holy about not knowing the Bible? Okay, so you know the Bible, but you just can't ask Him for anything because you're too holy.

We interrupt this chapter with a special offer for the over-holy people who just can't ask God for anything.

There are all kinds of so-called or self-proclaimed holy people. So we have for you a Holy Sewing Kit. It comes in assorted colors and flesh tones because if you've gone over holy, there's a breach somewhere and it's in your flesh, you need to let the Holy Spirit repair it.

- **Clear holy thread** - for the folk who don't see nobody because they think no one can see them in their ego trips. They don't speak, they don't really look at others. They think they're so holy they've gone invisible. They think they've been beamed up or about to be raptured, first. This thread comes in very light weight, as not to hinder the rapture that you expect to take place in your life.

- **White holy thread** - for obvious reasons, for the just saved, the just born again. The just baptized, the just washed clean because they are so clean. Having been washed and new that they know they will never sin again, and that's a bit too holy. They don't realize that this is the only the beginning of the Christian walk, not the end.

Don't be so hard on yourself. When Jesus reminds you that it is He who has saved you by Grace and that you are not saved by your own goodness and your own good works, God may remind you of that and in this Amazing Grace, right after you attempted sin, even in your salvation.

- **Blush holy thread** - for those embarrassed for people who are not as holy as they are, or think they are, they look down on the lowly ones, the spiritual peons, the ones who haven't appropriated the gifts of God, or real spiritual promises of God like they have. The ones that don't quote any Bible verses yet, as they do.

- **Brown holy thread** - for everyday over holy people who actually know a couple of Scriptures and believe they are henceforth little I AMS. They can tell you everything you did wrong up-to-the-minute, *in love*. There's a breech, baby. Something is out of order.

- **Dark brown holy thread** - for the privileged, holy, the high class holy. Those who are so pure they can be on vacation, at the beach, walking by the river, or even on the basketball court getting their tans on instead of in the House of God. And still they believe they are holy.

- **Black colored holy thread** - for those who self-righteousness and holiness are so severe they are living in complete and utter darkness. They believe just being *nice* will get them to Heaven. They believe being something such as an animal activist will get them to see God. I have a question: Where in the Bible is there any talk about animal rights? Folks were sacrificing animals right and left in the Old Testament.

When did God say stop? When we got the better covenant, surely. But when did God say that the animals should become your masters?

Sane man knows God never said that.

These colors are those who believe nice is all you need. Neither the Golden Rule, nor the Pledge of Allegiance will save anybody spiritually. Neither will baseball or apple pie.

And this color thread is for those who don't believe that God *IS*. And if you order right now, you can get the most sought-after color:

- **Gold Holy thread** - for those so holy they believe they're in their glorified body right now, or they think they have on their heavenly robes while still here on Earth. You can't get too close to these people. They believe they have personal angels carrying their trains of them golden robes, but in reality, nobody wants to get within 10 feet of them. Oh yes, the most important shade and unadvertised bonus free of charge.

- **Flesh tone holy thread** - this color is the perfect match to your flesh because if you think you're so holy then you are self-righteous and in your flesh. Our own righteousness is as filthy rags; sew up that whole before all of what's in you leaks out and smells up the place.

Don't refuse me, Lord because I'm too holy.

No, you're not. Be for real; ask God for the things you *really* want. Don't be afraid. He wants to give you such and such, and that's a whole lot of good stuff for your life and godliness. He won't refuse you.

Exercise:

Prayer:

21. Repent of lying.... I need to repent of these obvious lies. Use additional paper if necessary. Lies you tell God.
22. Lies you told yourself.
23. And I need to repent of these covert not so obvious lies.
24. What I really want or need from God spiritually.
    a. Financially.
    b. Emotionally.
    c. Relationships, socially and for my family.

d. Other Such as career, education or business.

Note that you will find that repenting from lies and lying will not only cleanse you, Your faith will increase when you finally begin to talk honestly to God about things in your heart and in your mind. Congratulations, this is how you build real relationship.

Stupid Money--*Money in Rebellion*

In today's slang, *stupid money* refers to having so much money that a person doesn't know what to do with it. It refers to suddenly having money, especially after having no money. It refers to an abundant overflow of discretionary and disposable funds that can be used any way a person chooses to use them. Stupid money.

I propose that money, whether it is a little or a lot, can be stupid. That's why you're in charge of it. That's why you're supposed to have access to Wisdom, to know what to do with money. Money is stupid and has no mind. That's why it can't be a *god*. Mammon is considered a little g *god* and it rules over money, but when I say money has no mind, I am referring to the paper and coins of financial exchange. Those inanimate objects have no mind, that's why it can't take care of you by itself. That's why it can't heal you. It can't get you healed. It can pay for healing that is in the scope of what doctors and medicine can do.

It can't buy you love. There you are smarter than money. At least you're supposed to be. That's why you have power and dominion *over* money.

Who's running the house, you or your kids? Who's running your life, you or your money?

Money that's doing what <u>it</u> wants to do instead of what God says for it to do is in rebellion.

Does your money want to go to the mall or bingo? Do you give in and take it where it wants to go? Maybe it likes to play the ponies, Paul said it was not himself but the sin in him that did the evil, (Romans 7:8). Is your money inviting you to sin or do unclean things that you really don't want to do, or will regret in the morning?

If this is your relationship with money, you are the type who will work for money. Money, with you as it's employee is not God's plan. Money obtained incorrectly, and lording over a life can wreck a life. That doesn't mean to run away from money; it means knock Mammon off the throne of your heart and put money in its proper place. Money is to serve you.

Is money speaking to the sin that used to be in your life that's supposed to be in remission--, is it calling it out? As deep speaks to deep, sin speaks to sin. When you don't have money or extra money, do you think on certain bad things to do when money is burning a hole in your pocket? If you think on bad things only when you have money, then money tempts you and leads you into temptation. **<u>YOU</u>** need to get control over money.

Spiritual Transference

Do you know where that money has been? Do you realize what the transference of *spirits* that money could be picking up spiritual things everywhere it goes and from every hand it touches? There are things and places you would never touch. There are activities that you should never engage in, places you would never let your children go, and you would not even let your pets go there, but you let your money go there and you don't think twice about it. You may not even wash your hands after touching money, in the natural.

How about your spiritual hands before and after handling money? Ever thought about that? Everybody has a spirit--, at least one. Too many people have a collection of spirits that influence, suggest, provoke, oppress, or possess them to do negative things that they may not, under normal circumstances, think of or do. Many of these things are acts you'd never think of doing yourself.

Or if you did think of them, you would have been delivered.

I wouldn't want to go back to thinking like that again. Spirits can transfer by touch and accumulate on surfaces to influence or take up residence in a person.

Aunt Bertie's Old ring was worth a fortune. She gave it to you in her will. Your life has been messed up ever since you first put it on. Even your health has suffered. Aunt Bertie had some occult secrets that you carried as bondages or curses when you begin wearing that ring.

Money is no different. It picks up spiritual stuff that can transfer.

I will now use the term bearer bonds, which really refers to a valuable certificate that entitles a person that holds it to be able to cash it and receive the value that's printed on it, in money. Like our green currency, whoever has it owns it. That's it. Well, spiritually, whoever has anything in their possession that carries a negative spiritual influence, or enchantment, it's called a charm. The wearer bears the bondage that comes with that enchanted item.

Don't be afraid. But when you're praying for that money to come out of those casinos and prostitution rings, from drug dealers, you better know how to **bless that money** to keep the spiritual dirt from getting on you and your family. You'd better know how to pray so that as you bear that money it doesn't put you in bonds.

To keep that spiritual dirt from transferring by simple touch or by holding it in your possession, on your person for prolonged periods of time, bless your money while the teller is counting it. Bless the change when the cashier is still figuring it out. Bless those dollar bills, bless those quarters, nickels, dimes and pennies too. We really don't know where they've been. It's not clean just because it's money. It's not blessed because it's money. It's not good just because it's money, and **it's not always from God just because it's money**.

The devil has money. The princedom of darkness has money. He lures people with it; he tempts people with it. He uses it for bogus deals that make the human think they'll get wealth, fame, riches, but later they find out that was a lie. It was a bait and switch.

He also has evil human agents in the Earth who facilitate these "deals."

If you knew the spiritual identity of the person who had just handed you that bag, handled that money or had it in his possession the longest, you might cringe. You might not want it. If they offered you their shoes, their clothes, or other items that they held an intimate position, you wouldn't want it unless you know that you know you have the power of God working for you to correct it spiritually and keep you spiritually safe from negative spiritual transference.

Money Working Against God

Money put to unclean use is working against God.

No matter what your money wants to do, it's up to you to manage it. Use it wisely and to the glory of God. It is up to you to make sure your money is being used properly according to the laws of God, especially if you want to work the principles of God. What are the laws of money? If you don't know, then you can't work them, but you are still responsible.

Before you knew about gravity, you were still responsible for falling if you stepped from the roof of a building. Just as you may not know the civil laws of the land if you break one, you're still responsible and accountable as if you had known it.

Money in Dominion

Money that is running the show has dominion over the person, instead of the person having dominion over money.

If you have ever said, *I can't do that, I don't have enough money* because you really don't have enough money, then money has dominion over you. If it's something you have to do, should do, need to do and can't do, the lack of money has been weaponized against you. If it's something you *want* to do that is not against God, you are still being held back, as in being under a curse.

Money that has dominion tells *you* what to buy, when to buy, for whom, and from whom. When money doesn't want you to buy something, it dries up and stops flowing like a child as though it's screaming, *"I'm not coming over anymore."* This has happened to countless first-time, tithers, sometimes making them one-time-only tithers. It is a control tactic of the devil. Money tells you when to give and when not to give.

Money represents your **life**. It is part of your worship. Whether you can open your mouth and sing, dance before the LORD or not, if the **physical sacrifice that represents your life** is not in the service, your worship has been thwarted or halted.

The Israelites did not go to worship God without their cattle. Cattle represented their money; it was their sacrifice. They did not go to worship without their wallets and checkbooks.

> Go and worship the LORD," he said. "But leave your flocks and herds here. You may even take your little ones with you." "No," Moses said, "you must provide us with animals for sacrifices and burnt offerings to the LORD our God.
> Exodus 10:24-28 NLT

When people walk in Dominion. Money does what they say do. Money serves them.

Money exalted as a *god*

When the Philistines stole the Ark of the Covenant, they put it in their treasure house next to the figure of their *god*. The image of their *god* Dagon fell over and broke to pieces next to the power of the presence of God and the Ark, (1

Samuel 5:2-7). **Thou shalt not have any God before me,** (Exodus 20:3). The money *god*, Mammon has fallen and will fall when it is placed beside your God, Jehovah. But if Jehovah is never put in approximation to Mammon, it won't fall. If the Word of God is never applied to situations where you seem to be favoring the money *god* over the Only Living God, how will you know how they compare? But God says, **if you put them before Me, I will show you who's really God.**

Jehovah can still knock over Mammon, the money *god* any day of the week.

How many times have you made the excuse, I can't do that, I don't have enough money when you really do have plenty of money. How many times have you *not* been willing to part with certain sums of money or the last of your money, even at God's instruction? If that's you, your trust is in the money, not in God.

How many have you used the *no money* excuse to get out of doing something, going somewhere, or sharing--, even with your own children? If you can't stand the thought of not having a certain amount of money in your hand, or in your checking account, then money is limiting your life. You have money, but you are trusting in money. I don't mean you have to live in doubt, poverty or lack, but if you have never experienced God filling your pockets or your accounts, then you've never experienced Jehovah Jireh, Our Provider.

If you cannot be led by God, to give sacrificially so He can reveal Himself to you, and bless others, then money is your *god*.

Whether you submit that money to God willingly or not, there will come a time when He shows you, He's Jehovah and no other God will come before Him. Your little money *god* will be defeated. Completely.

Money Put Before God

If you think like this: *God can get His money, but I need this, I really need this. I can't put this in the offering,* then you should ask God if you are valuing money over Him and His purposes. I hope you've never said that, though. **When the offering plate/basket of atonement for your sins was passed, God put Jesus in it, not a $10 bill crumpled up and sweaty because He didn't want to let it go.** Look what He gave you. Jesus. A high blessing and Salvation in Jesus Christ, as well as the Holy Spirit.

Unsaved Money

Unsaved money is not the money that is not in a savings account or mutual fund. What if your money, where it is now, and where it goes, were presented at the White Throne judgment? Give your money a life for a moment. Give it personality. Listen closely as it tries to explain its comings and its goings, its choices and its sins.

Money, where have you been?

Money might respond. *"Oh, I've been everywhere. You name it, I've traveled. I've been here and there--, everywhere, bars, strip joints, casinos, crack houses, adult bookstores, horse races, Bingo--, everywhere, living my best life."*

When asked if they've been to church, only a few dollars might raise their hands. Then the money will blame you, *"God, that man or woman you gave me would not take me to church or wouldn't put me in the church's Offering."* And ultimately, you are responsible and accountable for where your money goes. Your money will not account for you on Judgment Day. **You** must *give* account for it.

Unconsecrated Money

There is no money that arrives in your hand already consecrated. Each hand that receives it has to consecrate it unto the LORD and for godly purposes and service.

If you don't bring the tithe into the House of God to be blessed, then your money is *unconsecrated.* If some of it is not set aside to be consecrated, then **all** of it is **cursed**. If it is unblessed, unsanctified money, it will never go as far as it could if the tithe had been paid back to God, and consecrated. It will not last as long as it could, it will not bless as it should, and you may find it hard to hold on to in the now and in the future. The devil (Mammon) is *in* unconsecrated money, he is the prince of this world, and he just tags along onto every dollar bill. Unconsecrated savings and investments may suffer. God has set a way for you to avoid financial disaster that the world will suffer, because the worlds system will fail. God has established this principle to bless you.

Stubborn Money

Stubborn money won't allow you to give it or sow it.

Have you ever met people who really, really want to give, but they just can't seem to? They leave their purses and checkbooks in the car, or at home. They just can't bring themselves to tithe or give offerings. It's almost painful and grievous for them to think of giving anything, especially money. It's almost as though that money is talking to them, screaming, *"Keep me, keep me, do anything but don't send me to church. Don't leave me in the offering."* That's Mammon trying to block your worship.

You got some of that kind of money. All of us have run across some of it at some time or other. It's the money that's used to being at the mall, so it wants to go back there. Some of that money is used to being in the hands of the crack dealer, so it wants to go back there and live a thug's life. It is the money that's used to being at the casino, it wants to go back there--, I mean they have free drinks.

Just as some people don't want to come to church because of the *spirit* of the anti-Christ that sits on their hearts, there is money that has been living in miserly pockets for so long that in addition to having the *spirit* of Mammon on it, it has also picked up the *spirit* of its long-term owner. Or it may have had many owners--, all in the *world*. They want to keep that money in the world because they know when it gets into the hands of a Christian, when it gets into a tithing envelope or an offering plate, then touched by the power of God, that it will not want to come out into the world again. But this kind of money, won't cooperate in the House of God until it is **consecrated** and **sanctified**, until it is taught its place and purpose. That's what the touch does.

Money That Won't Multiply

Ignorant money. Money has a spirit, but it does not have a mind. We are spirit, but we are also have a mind that we're supposed to be renewed in. We're to seek Wisdom and understanding and to not be ignorant. Do you have any idea how dumb and stupid your money is? If you lay it down somewhere, it just lays there. If it falls out of your pocket, it doesn't let you know it fell. It doesn't seem to know its way back home when you leave it somewhere, and it doesn't alert you when someone is trying to steal it from you. It has no loyalty. It just goes along, no matter if someone is trying to take it, or even if someone is trying to take it to ungodly places.

Money doesn't know how to add itself, to subtract itself, or divide itself, and money definitely does not know how to multiply itself, but God does. Money is not smart enough to automatically multiply itself. It needs help. For these reasons and others. You can't ask your money what it wants to do. **You have to tell it.**

We've been discussing the Parable of the Penny (Matthew 20:1-16). Three different people went out to do a certain job at three different times of day, but they all earned the same amount of money. Why? They earn the amount of money that they agreed to earn for the time worked. In the spiritual this is a good thing that we all receive Salvation and Eternal Life no matter what time we enter into God's marvelous Light, whether as a child, a teen, in midlife, or even later. But when it comes to money, money may have you working too hard for too little of it. Again, who's in control of your money, you or your money? You've got to be smart enough to have the money come to you for work you've done. We don't work solely for money but do work for profit, we expect increase, and we deserve the fruits of our labor. But **it is the work itself that is the worship, and that honors and glorifies God.**

What you agree to earn reflects what you think you're worth. If you think you're worth $10 per hour, that's what you'll agree to. But the person next to you may be thinking they are worth $15 or $20 an hour. But if you agree to $10 per hour, you have no issue with your coworker or employer. You have made covenant of sorts to work 40 hours a week for so many dollars per hour. Money won't tell you based on how long and hard you work for it, how much you should earn. You may earn the most money you have ever made in your life for doing the thing that is the easiest work that you've ever done in your life. Harder work does not necessarily mean more money. It should, but money is not that smart, so you have to be.

When you go out into the world to work, you take certain things with you such as your mind, your skills, your knowledge, your physical ability, your experiences. Most often, you take almost everything you have with you to earn some money. Seems like the more stuff you have to take, the more gifts, talents, skills, abilities you have to use on the job the more money you should make--, not necessarily *if you work for money*. But money doesn't know that. Money is not that smart, so you have to be.

Don't work for money. Do not work for money only. Make money come to you and work for you. It is your servant.

God doesn't want you to have unblessed money.

Money That Won't Bless Others

Selfish money, money that will not bless others, is like a seedless grape. It will never multiply, and it will only be eaten, consumed, or wither and die. This kind of money has been in the presence of and handled by some very selfish and probably worldly people. However, there are some professed Christians who need deliverance from selfishness. That money you're holding could have been in anybody's hands, even a very selfish person. Do you want to keep it on you long enough for that *spirit of selfishness* to transfer to you? Get that accursed thing out of your camp before it corrupts the rest of your money, or you find yourself not wanting to go to church because you don't want to give. Hurry, get that money where it belongs, in the Offering before you start reciting the lie, *"All the preacher wants is your money."*

You aren't one of those people who comes into church 45 minutes or an hour after service has begun thinking the Offering has already been taken, are you?

I met a lovely and spiritually gifted young woman bootlegging at a women's conference. She got all she could out of the meeting until the offering was announced. Then she was nowhere to be seen, and it wasn't even her church's conference. Maybe she didn't have any money. Maybe, probably the case. She is well-employed, has a full-time job with good benefits, but appears to spend every cent on her clothes, hair and appearance. She's exhibiting a *form* of godliness.

God is not pleased, and I was embarrassed and grieved for her.

Dirty Dollars

Do you want money? Surely you do. Dr Marlene, you're describing money as something awful and dirty. The tangible currency *is* dirty. It's been in sweaty hands, linty pockets, junky purses, on floors, worn in shoes, on the ground, even up some noses. Grandma might have kept a stash of cash down her blouse for all we know. Naturally it can be washed, and spiritually, thank God, it can be washed too. If you acquire it and never wash it, you'll be subject to the germs that are on it. How about *spiritual* germs that remain on your money? You've got to bless those dollar bills and consecrate them in church by tithing.

Disobedient Money

Money that goes to the mall, skipping church, money that goes to the casino, money that goes to dinner and sporting events but will not go to church is disobedient money. Money is like a child that needs to be disciplined. It needs to be trained and made to do what it's supposed to do. Undisciplined money is unchurched money,

money that has been everywhere and anywhere, picking up anything and everything. You've got to take Dominion and authority over this money. The first thing you have to do is tithe. Then you give offerings and charitable donations and gifts. You cannot skip the first step.

Knock Mammon Off the Throne

Every time you get money, Mammon creates the temptation to make a covenant with it instead of making or maintaining your covenant with God. Every time you get money Mammon tries to climb onto the throne of your heart.

People who work for the love of money are carnal. There may be a time in your life that you *have* to work a job that you hate because of certain dire circumstances, such as you need to provide for a family. But folks who work at a job they hate simply for the love of money and will do ***anything*** for money. Those are carnal people.

A carnal man is dangerous. He is at risk of becoming an agent of Satan because he will do anything for money, fame, wealth, success, one upmanship—revenge. Anything.

A person who will do ***anything*** for money is serving Mammon as their *god*. Anything. Meaning the sacrifice of their will, morals, goals, soul—even the sacrifice of others is not off their radar, although they may not yet know it. They just know THEY want something and that THEY want it so badly that it doesn't matter what anyone else thinks or wants – it doesn't matter about anyone else, just them.

A love for God correlates to a love for people. A person who can't love people, who doesn't love people, who really can't love anyone, but self is a DANGEROUS person.

In any type of relationship, especially a close, interpersonal relationship, a person will treat you the way they treat God. A man who doesn't love God – well, baby, you're taking a huge chance.

Consecrated Money

They say of the dying that once they see God, they don't want to come back. When that money sees what it could be, what it should be, when it arrives at the feet of God, the Throne of God, and finds out its real purpose it will want to serve God, and in serving God, that money will want to serve you. Money is subject to the heart of the owner of that money.

But it's only money, you may say. Unblessed means cursed, and cursed means not blessed. Another bold Dr. Marlene statement. Is it really true? Does unblessed mean cursed?

Yes?

Is it also true that unblessed people are cursed? You answer this one.

Consecration Prayer

I bless my dollar bills, in the Name of Jesus.

Lord, give me enough to be satisfied so I don't get fat in my comforts, or have to steal just to eat. Grow me where I need to be growing so you can bless me to the full extent that you've always planned to bless me. Help me to be the me that You've always planned me to be, in Jesus' Name, Amen.

Financial Terrorism

Do you want to mix your money, *which represents your life*, with someone whose life is in rebellion against God? Have you ever thought of the ramifications of that? Would you fund a terrorist group? No. Although we should profit and make a profit in the system we are in (the world's system) we are wise to acknowledge God in our investment choices. In the Parable of the Talents we learn that we can put our money to the money changers to make a profit because profitable servants are pleasing to God.

I would love to exclusively spend my money with Christians who are Kingdom building, but that isn't always possible. Sometimes a worldly boutique may be the only one with the dress you want. Even if you sew, the shop with an unsaved shop owner may be the only one with the fabric and notions, you need to make your own clothes. So we keep going into the world because we live in the world.

Each trip into the world could be an evangelistic adventure if you allow yourself to be used of God, or it could be a treacherous trip of worldly contamination. It depends on how you handle yourself. Maybe the unsaved fabric store owner needs to be witnessed to.

If we could only work for Christians, that would be great. Many of us go into the world daily, to earn a living. Even so, the money we earn is not automatically consecrated just because an employer professes Christianity. There are Christians who don't bless the food they are about to eat, every day, so you know they probably don't bless (consecrate) their money.

What happens when you keep dipping in a bag of potting soil? Your hands get dirty, right? What happens when you keep dipping your hands into the world to get money? Hands may also get dirty, so:

Bless those dollar bills.

Yeah, you're begging God to give you money, increase your salary, and give you promotion at your job. Are you asking God to give you more of His consecrated money to mix with your unconsecrated money? God hates mixtures. Sanctify your money as God told you, and He'll not refuse you.

*God, I know I haven't blessed my money, so my money is not clean. My know my hands are not clean, my motives are selfish, but would You give me some more money? Will You mix Your holy money with mine so I can live comfortably and continue doing what **I** want? I don't think I have enough to tithe. And even if I did, well, You know about that preacher…*

*So anyway, Lord, if you want me to give **me** an offering or something, I'll just slip my mother 50 bucks, my dad 50 bucks, then You'll see what a good person I am…. And you can bless me, Lord.*

If you are honest, you might admit that this is your unspoken prayer. God can't honor that kind of attitude and plans.

It's Ours

Money should be so blessed that when people in the world put their hands on it and have it in their possession, *it should bless them*. It should encourage them to do right. It should even draw them to the Kingdom of holiness, like Paul's healing handkerchiefs--, it should *heal* them. It should deliver them. Money is a very common point of contact. Christians should have blessed it all by now and people should be clamoring for it not for the power it wields in the Earth, but for the Grace and anointing on it. But then again, the currency is filled with satanic symbols, if you only take a look. That is all the more reason to bless it, bless it, bless it when it comes into your possession.

However, we should be more concerned that money doesn't contaminate us. How many do reckless things, or act in unbecoming ways when they get money?

Christians, the other side seems to have no problem putting enchantments on anything, really. They pray over stuff they want to sell so they can make either a lot of money in business, or so their evil agenda will be propagated in the Earth. What do we do? Make a product and *hope* for the best? Why is prayer such a problem for Christians, but those who practice dark arts will stay up and chant all night?

We serve the King of Glory – it don't take all night, but what's wrong with prayer? We must humble ourselves and pray for ourselves, our families, for the Kingdom of God and this whole world.

We in the Kingdom of God should have it all, and we should have control over all the money in the world. Yes, I said that if money is used as a weapon *against* us, then we should have control over all of it in spoils, in our spiritual warfare. We should be acquiring all the money, **all the enemy's weapons** and deactivating the power in them so they cannot be used against us anymore. Those weapons include *their* money. We should be accessing it and *consecrating* it.

If money is not in any other category, it's *such and such*. And God says He'll give us the desires of our heart, even *such and such*.

Terrorists include those who are fluent in disobedience and insurgency. If you are in rebellion, it's against Him. Do you think God is going to fund terrorism against *Himself*? No, of course not. The sane man says, *No*.

You need to get radical, not rebellious regarding your beliefs about money. First of all, you should *have* some beliefs, not just what you've heard, what you think, or what your parents and grandparents may have shared with you. What do *you* believe? Read the Bible and seek the face of God and find out what you should know and what should be your attitude about money.

Don't refuse me, Lord. Show Him you know how to control yourself and exert dominion over money, and He will hear your petition and bless you abundantly.

Exercise:

25. Identify your money. Is most of my money
    a. Rebellious or obedient, cooperative or stubborn?
    _____
    _____
    b. Clean or unclean?
    _____

26. Use the headings in this chapter to identify your money. _____
_____

27. I aspire for my money to be:
_____

28. I bless what? _____ _____ _____

Financial Warfare

Financial warfare doesn't have anything to do with the corner gas station octane prices. Financial warfare is spiritual warfare about your finances, your money, and your *stuff*. Tearing down spiritual strongholds may involve the breaking and destroying of generational curses, bondages, and yokes. Sometimes you may have felt overwhelmed by money troubles that may have beset you, but because of the volume or how critical the situation is, you may have thought, *What in the world did I do to cause any of this?*

Truth is you may not have done anything to cause it. But since you noticed, since you mentioned it, since you are now uncomfortable enough to want relief or remedy, since God now has your attention, let's do something about it.

The actions of the lifetimes of 30 or more people you may not have ever met may have caused the financial woes you are now experiencing. You're praying to God, but it seems that He is refusing you. Who are these 30 or more people, and their 30 lifetimes who have *anything* to do with your finances? While it's not your boss at work, it's not your banker, and it's not necessarily your spouse, but it could be. Predominantly it's *your* relatives, *your* parents, grandparents on both sides, whether you know them or even know who they are. And possibly your great grandparents on both your mother's and your father's sides of your family--, whether you know them or even know who they are.

Now that you're married, consider your spouse's folks, too. You did agree to the better and the worse. The answers may have made your bed, and now you're tossing and turning in it. You can't sleep--, got too many financial problems on your mind.

What Have They Done?

Well, I don't know. You may not know either, but you can know by asking questions of those who are still with you. When you receive salvation and God's Spirit, you can ask the Holy Spirit. The Holy Spirit may not reveal the sordid details, or the desperate dastardly deeds committed or acts of ignorance, but He will reveal to you what you need to pray. Seek after Wisdom. Read your Bible where it talks about curses and find out what things God has cursed; not what man has cursed. You will probably need to ask the Holy Spirit, because most people try to keep sins a secret.

After you get the spiritual map, then stand in a spiritual armor (Ephesians 6) and do warfare against them all, each one. You may feel a check or knowing in your spirit if it applies to you and your family history. As you pray, you will feel the release, a lifting or freedom as God delivers you from these oppressions. Continue to seek Wisdom. Read books, listen to tapes, messages, and sermons on the subject, then the Lord will give you a knowing or a sense of urgency to pray about things that affect your spiritual situation today.

Poverty is a spirit, but wealth is a Power.

Claire, while reading a book that just piqued her curiosity, came across a section on the demonic devastation of Freemasonry. It was only mildly interesting at first, but then the Holy Spirit gave her vision of a freemasons apron that was her father's. She remembered it as a flashback, based on the description given in the book. Her father had not been in that activity for over 35 years and the memory was not a significant part of her childhood days. But the Holy Spirit will bring all things back to your remembrance, she remembered as a child of five or six years old, seeing that apron, looking at the images on it and wondering why her father, and not her mother had an apron since her dad didn't cook. At all. At that time, she didn't even know what a Freemason was, but that image had stayed in her subconscious mind for decades. The Holy Spirit then brought it to her remembrance at a time when she had enough information, knowledge, understanding and spiritual foundation to know what to do. This may sound very complicated, but the event which our primitive words describe took only seconds. Then Claire had to make a decision and take action. She took spiritual authority in order to reverse her situation.

Take Authority

You now have authority over all these *unclean spirits* and oppressing demons in the name of Jesus. If you have discovered that the thief has stolen anything from you, now you have to take authority by the blood of Jesus and the Word of God to renounce demonic covenants made in your family's bloodline, even before you were born. Take authority. Be bold. If you don't have the boldness or assurance, seek wise counsel, and intercessory warriors to do spiritual battle for you or with you. If you're going to into financial warfare, then it's about those dollar bills, honey. It's about substituting what God intended or what the devil implemented. It's time to do spiritual warfare by binding and *loosing*. Public concerns and abundant wealth, financial security and welfare.

But, if he be found, he should restore sevenfold, and he shall give all the substance of his house, (Proverbs 6:31).

How Did This Happen?

I know God didn't recreate the Garden at Eden every year, and I'm pretty sure He didn't recreate it every Spring. Much of God's other seed will multiply on its own unless you stop it by sin, disobedience, rebellion, or other flesh acts. Grace promotes grace. Faith promotes faith. Strength leads to more strength, honor--, honor, love--, love, mercy--, mercy…. Unless stopped by sin, rebellion, or disobedience, the blessings that God intended will flow from generation to generation. Get the picture?

Have you ever planted flowers in your yard that came back the following year without replanting? Many things were like that in the world and in the Kingdom of God. What you give out comes back to you and many times what you plant keeps on giving.

In generational matters, what you and those in your family who came before you planted may keep coming back for years and years. Generational curses keep repeating, visiting the 3rd and 4th generations. The great-great grandchild may not have done anything other than be *born* into a family, where a certain sin was sown, yet that child, and you have to share in the iniquity of that sin.

How can any of us, except by amnesia go to visit a newborn descendant in our family and not think of the spiritual doors we've opened that will be stumbling blocks or curses for that darling newborn? Doors that we need to shut or should have shut as soon as we heard that child was on the way. Doors we need to definitely shut before we die. As much as it inconveniences us but for the love of that unsuspecting child and all of our generations.

Families who practice black arts know what their offspring are being birthed into and they are proud of it for the most part.

Christians please. Especially those who have accepted salvation but are still sinning. You're living a dangerous existence. You can't just sin until you want to stop just because you got saved and baptized when you were 13.

When you get older and hopefully wiser and can't sin anymore or decide to finally stop, you can't just *forget* about sin; you've got to **repent**. Yeah, stop sinning, but you've got work to do. Repent. Renounce the sin. Renounce evil covenants made. Break soul ties. Break curses that are the result of evil covenants made. Bind demons enforcing the curses down your bloodline. Bind strongmen and retaliation down your bloodline. And you may need to break evil altars (Exodus 34:13), tearing them down in the spirit. With that much work to undo the results of sin, why sin? It's just not worth it. **Woe to those who are at ease in Zion, those who think that when you are through with sin, you can set it down**

like the bones of a hot wing that you've eaten all the meat off of. Nope.

Iniquity, like a perennial can be self-perpetuating in its bondage. But thank God **blessings** are also passed on from father to son. The father sows the blessing. Generation to generation can reap of the favor, blessings and grace of God because it is passed on. Most families are very conscious, or should be, to pass on the blessings, but many don't know how to stop the curses from transferring.

Poverty is a *spirit*

If your finances are adversely affected, knowing what sins lead to poverty is very useful. First thing you want to rule out, that it's not you. Poverty comes on by gossip, slothfulness, laziness, observing the wind, (Eccl 11:4). It comes on by ignorance, the occult, and other **sin**. It is transferred the same way all spirits are transferred, by blood, generationally, by relationship and association. Even if you don't associate with certain "broke" relatives, you are still related by blood. Pray for a new spiritual connection, hooked up into the family of God. Be connected by the

Blood of Jesus. Because you love your folks, you can help them become transfused with this New Blood also. And they can be set free from the bondage of financial defeat and worry, as well as other generational curses. Not by giving them money, necessarily, but hooking them up with Salvation through Jesus Christ.

Wealth is a Power

Wealth comes from obedience, worship, tithing, diligence and giving offerings to God. It comes from being in right order, under authority, and in submission. The Power to get wealth is a gift from God. It is a High Blessing. Job experienced the High Blessing of great wealth from God from the beginning, and then after the devastation, he was restored back into wealth and prosperity. The Word teaches us that even if we've had wealth in the past and don't have it now, no matter what we've been through, God is still able and willing to bless us mightily again. The latter rain is greater than the former as long as we are in right relationship and in order with Him.

Wellth

Wellth is a word I just coined and it's driving spellcheck crazy. All the blessings of God are not material, they are not all monetary. Sometimes, you need good success, joy, peace, and happiness. Sometimes you need healing in your body. Sometimes you need your child to come in off the street, or that man to stop beating you and get a job. Sometimes you need demonic interference, oppression, possession, lifted, broken, bound up, cast out of your household and your family.

Sometimes you need deliverance and salvation for loved ones. It's not all about money; sometimes you need understanding on which way to go and how to get there, sometimes you need a good night's sleep. You want to be able to say, *It is well with my soul.*

You want to be able to represent the presence and the *wellth* of God to onlookers. You want your lifestyle to draw people, not to repel them from the Kingdom of God and the church. Wealth is something for which I would implore God. Don't refuse me, Lord, I am asking for all the blessings **and** *wellth*; I am sure He will not refuse me. It may not be instantaneous, but as my soul prospers, I will make room to receive; and He will bless me.

You should walk in all the ways which the Lord your God hath committed you. That he may live, that he may live. And that it may be well worth you. And that you may prolong your days in the land which you shall possess. (Deuteronomy 5:33)

Exercise:

Generational curses and strongholds to tear down:

1. _____
2. _____
3. _____
4. _____

Amen.

Dear Reader:

Thank you for reading this volume. May it enlighten you and may the Lord bless you in every way, in the Name of Jesus. Amen.

Dr. Marlene Miles has served in ministry for 20+ years. She is a prayer warrior, Christian author and speaker. Her topics include prayer, spiritual warfare, deliverance, relationships and finance. She also writes children's books that are available on amazon, Kindle and many other platforms.

Enjoy revelatory messages on the Dr Miles Youtube channel. Pray along with the Warfare Prayer Channel also on Youtube.

Christian books by this author

AK: Adventures of the Agape Kid

AMONG SOME THIEVES

As My Soul Prospers

Behave

Churchzilla (The Wanna-Be Bride of Christ)

The Coco-So-So Correct Show

Demons Hate Questions

Devil Weapons: *Anger, Unforgiveness & Bitterness*

Do Not Orphan Your Seed

Do Not Work for Money

Don't Refuse Me Lord

The FAT Demons

got Money?

Let Me Have a Dollar's Worth

Living for the NOW of God

Lord, Help My Debt

Lose My Location

Made Perfect In Love

The Man Safari *(Really, I'm Just Looking)*

Marriage Ed., *Rules of Engagement & Marriage*

The Motherboard: *Key to Soul Prosperity*

Name Your Seed

Plantation Souls

The Poor Attitudes of Money

Power Money: Nine Times the Tithe

The Power of Wealth

Seasons of Grief

Seasons of War

SOULS in Captivity

Soul Prosperity: Your Health & Your Wealth

The *spirit* of Poverty

The Throne of Grace, *Courtroom Prayers*

Time Is of the Essence

Triangular Powers (4 book series)

Warfare Prayer Against Poverty

When the Devourer is Rebuked

The Wilderness Romance

<u>Other Journals & Devotionals by this author</u>:

The Cool of the Day – **Journal**

got HEALING? Verses for Life

got HOPE? Verses for Life

got GRACE? Verses for Life

got JOY? Verses for Life

got PEACE? Verses for Life

got LOVE? Verses for Life

He Hears Us, Prayer Journal *4 colors*

I Have A Star, **Dream Journal** *kids, teen, adult*

I Have A Star, **Guided Prayer Journal**,

J'ai une Etoile, Journal des Reves

Let Her Dream, Dream Journal

Men Shall Dream, Dream Journal,

My Favorite Prayers (in 4 styles)

My Sowing Journal (in three different colors)

Tengo una Estrella, Diario de Sueños

<u>**Illustrated children's books by this author:**</u>

Big Dog (8-book series)

Do Not Say That to Me

Every Apple

Fluff the Clouds

I Love You All Over the World

Imma Dance

The Jump Rope

Kiss the Sun

The Masked Man

Not During a Pandemic

Push the Wind

Tangled Taffy

What If?

Wiggle, Wiggle; Giggle, Giggle

Worry About Yourself

You Did Not Say Goodbye to Me

www.ingramcontent.com/pod-product-compliance
Lightning Source LLC
LaVergne TN
LVHW052032080426
835513LV00018B/2293